I Looked Upon A Star

Faizaan Khan

BookLeaf Publishing

India | USA | UK

Dedication

"For my parents, sisters and friends whose unwavering love and support made this possible."

\-

"Dedicated to my beloved star whose passion and love runs through my blood and is reflected in my poetry."

Preface

"I looked upon a star", A tempest of emotions unfolds in these pages. These poems are born when your love grows through intensity; unraveling those fine threads of attraction, infatuation, dedication, prayer and passion. From the intoxicating inferno of passion to the icy depths of heartbreak, this collection is a raw and unflinching exploration of the human soul. Yearning and longing intertwine with promises broken and trust shattered. A delicate balance between love and hate, hope and despair, is meticulously explored, revealing the complexities of the human heart with searing intensity.

Acknowledgements

To my beloved star, I would like to express my deepest gratitude to you, your inspiration, intense love, and unwavering belief in me have been the driving force behind this work. Your passion ignited a fire within me that brought my words to life.

To my parents, whose unconditional love and sacrifices have laid the foundation for everything I am. To my sisters, for their constant support and companionship. To my friends, for their unwavering loyalty and encouragement.

A special thanks to my furry companion, Momo, whose purrs and cuddles provided much-needed comfort and inspiration during the writing process.

I am eternally grateful to my teachers, whose wisdom and guidance have ignited my passion for knowledge. And to the countless strangers who have, unknowingly, imparted invaluable life lessons, shaping me into the person I am today.

Your influence has been instrumental in this work, and I dedicate it to all of you with heartfelt appreciation. And to all the readers who support me, your enthusiasm means the world.

I looked upon a star

I looked upon a star in the whole galaxy, it would come every night.
I spoke to it one day. Why would you tease me?
It said someone sent me, you can't be alone on these nights.
It never gave a strong light through but soothed my soul.
And a time came where it vanished so suddenly that I couldn't look up to it.

*Don't know where it came from
or who sent it.*

*I feel nothing. Nothing bothers
me, except for the fact of thee.
I can't forget the days of purity
that existed.
All that is left are now the pieces
of memories
Voices that were guests are now
the owners, they rule unjust and
unfair.
Everything now perceived is just
an imagination.*

*There is nothing true nor is
anything false.
Believe what you want.
I thought I could get a hold of
myself.
Instead, my heart melted.
It burns away with a flick of
endless hope.
To be fulfilled, to be loved.
Wonder if they regret what took
place in a galaxy the black hole
of grief*

*I see no hope. Under lies my
fears.*

There's still darkness beneath my
tears.
Or so why am I?
Supposed to be righteous
Or am I supposed to be
courageous?
I can't pull on that dread with a
smile.
To my demise ends my patience.
Who knows what lies beneath, I
wonder tales of grief.
What's left to hear are nothing
but my own silenced thoughts.
Everyday drives a new pain,
My life is full of stain.
Grasses of drought,

Broken glasses cannot be sought.
My admiration is just a vain
space,
Looked upon a star in a galaxy of
grief

Amazed by your presence

Amazed by your presence I recall

Decided to give my heart for

once and all

As I remember the act of

pretending

Never knew that you would be so

interesting

How carefully your lips moved I

observed

Words replicated pearls I admired

Passionately as we moved

furthermore

The way we got to know each
other more
Never have you left from me
Never have I left from thee
I have seen those dark stillness
Around them covering their own
illness
But never have I ever
experienced
The same over you referenced
There is something about you
extraordinary
A spark of resilience to never be
ordinary

Unexpected Arrival

for your arrival i would decorate

the night

ask sun to calm and moon to

embrace

order clouds to change their

appearance

and rivers to be smooth as glide

I would distinguish heat from the

fire

Coldness from the snow

And would present them in an

attire

So beautiful that your cheeks
would blush
Colourful your eyes will make
them glow
For your arrival i would decorate
the night
Ask breeze to float cool and low
Halt time and make it dance
Songs of aeons and delight
I would hold your delicate hands
And fall in love with you again
The hearts entwined yet are apart
To my despair the night never
last

My Beloved Star

I would sneak you away from the

pinnacle of time

Oh my beloved star i would only

love you

Heart wrenching yet still

conscious of prime

In a shadowed realm, the only

light i find is you

You favours upon me with your

such adore

My love for you, infinite and

eternally divine

Your voice humming, my desire

to hear more

In a cosmic realm, i reside at the

center star of mine

Let the skies and heavens cluster

up and die

The cosmic and shadow realms

seize to exist

I am a soul of endearment, I

would for you standby

Till the new birth and the

beginning of time exist

My Guiding Star

She's a delicate soul, with dreams to unfold,
A heart full of hope, with stories untold.
Her spirit is free, with a gentle might,
A shining star, on a cloudy night.

Her heart is a canvas, of emotions so bright,

A changeable cloud, with shades of light.
Sometimes a sunbeam, that shines so free,
Sometimes a tempest, whispering secrets to me.

With a straightforward heart, and a gentle grace,
She navigates life, with a quiet pace.
Lost in her thoughts, with a timid stride,
But love blooms when she acts, with a heart full of pride.

Why did she come to me? Like a missing piece,
As if she's a part of me, a heartfelt release.
No one understands her, like I do,
A sweet, lovely girl, with a heart so true.

A crazy girl, lost in dreams so wide,
Wondering what's next, with a heart full of pride.
I want to make all her dreams come true,

And be the safe haven, where her heart can renew.

Not every relative, understands her way,
Not everyone sees, the beauty she display.
But I do, with a love so strong and free,
I'm addicted to her, like a melody.

She's the light of my eyes, my guiding star,
She's become my heartbeat, near and far.

I want to tell her, how much I adore,
And cherish her forever, like a precious score.

Your name

I steal moments from the time,
my love,
For you, my heart beats with
fervent desire.
This deceitful heart, it knows no
reason,
Blindly, it loves the darkness, the
fire.
Why do you ask what I'd like to
say?
Even in death, my love for you
would stay.

*Your voice, a melody that gently
hums,*
*A wanderer, I love this madness
of mine.*
*Let earth and sky vanish, let me
be undone,*
*A soul I am, loving this soul of
thine.*
*How can I look away from these
eyes of yours,*
*From which such love endlessly
pours?*
*This love for you is extreme, it's
true,*
*It hurts, it torments, it's nothing
new.*

*My heart now beats for you, my
dear,
Your story is all I care to hear.
Come, my companion, let us
journey so,
Your safety is my only vow.
Though you may complain, it's
only fair,
For such devotion, grace I
declare.
Your name, a prayer, I'll recite,
Oh, love, my heart's delight.*

AS I STEP OUT IN THIS WORLD

as i step out in this world i see

those remarkable visionaries to

me

i wonder why these exist of all

each different as i move and

recall

that sun which glares at me in

anguish

mocks me at my vanquish

i despair waiting for a deceiver

the moon as i call it a reliever

for that they betrays me

everytime

as i step out in this world i see

those fake expressions that

carries me

happiness is a questionable

emotion

for to those who has compassion

this void realm of darkness

engulfing thoughts and madness

all among find tranquility

for the less do they know truly

the peace lies in someone's love

as I step out in this world I see

those clouds of endless hope

pretending to rain across the
globe
carrying uneasiness as they
travel
for sure there are things yet
unravel
i feel like a traveler, a journey to
chase
the journey i want to embrace
sometimes i question life in itself
it answers me partial and hides
itself
as i step out in this world i see
a rejuvenated soul, my charm
gazing me and holding my palm

thoughts buzzing like bees
around honey
dreams of her became mine and
many
i see the eyes of yours as if they
are stars
only to find galaxies beyond
those stars
who would find peace in a
person they ask
chuckling i replied why not
remove that mask
as i step out in this world i see
Sparkling vision of yours radiates
through me
And it's as if you could see

That I carry the smile you gave

Upon my lips always that you have

Your breath became the essence of my existence

I can't bear to live more without your presence

You exactly fit right through me inside

I will be for you and you be my beside

as I step out in this world I see

Enriched feelings embodied personification

And the fact it is my satisfaction

Looking around I ponder over
you
I follow relying my heart upon
you
Silenced thoughts provokes my
inner self
To the extent where I see myself
Acceptance is of regards to you
my love
Attaining peace in the arms of
you my love
As I step out in this world I see

But..........

You made us a promise and now you want to leave?

You took my heart already and now you want to leave?

You think it's better and now you want to leave?

You made me a human and now you want to leave?

You taught me how to love and now you want to leave?

You took my hand in yours and now you want to leave?

You held me in your arms and now you want to leave?
You touched my soul and made it yours and now you want to leave?

But

When you promised us I promised you
When you took my heart I gave it to you
When you think it's better I'm with you

*When you made me human I
became one for you
When you taught me how to love
I loved you
When you took my hand in
yours I simply gave it to you
When you held me around your
arms I covered you
When you touched my soul and
made it yours I named it after
you*

Why the way it is

I'm lethargically broken down
Falsely accused and blamed on
My own betrayed me
My one hates me
I wonder what crime I did
I question myself what I did
Are they really my own?
Or are they really my enemies?
Pretending as if everyone cares
I'm scoffing because no one cares

But what happened to your heart
Why can't it hear my heart
Why is it deafen on rumours?
Why doesn't it trust the love of
ours?
I'm confused and amazed as
such
The tragedy occurred believing
true to such
I don't know what to do now
I'm crying heavily Inside now
I realized I was living in between
snakes
Poisoned are there minds and the
lives they takes

*The one I found home in lives
here too
Thought the home safe but they
poisoned it too*

*I plead oh! my Lord I'm innocent
I beg please save me and my
home this second
I'm a broken joy trying to smile
My wound swells and mind
senile
I wonder why it is the way it is
But my love for you will always
be the way it is*

You became

Rebellious how the fate became

The moment a part of me that

you became.

Through time and time managed

to get a hold

Of you, the farthest of stars that

you became.

My eyes that captured a

charming face once

It shows a replay of my Charm

that you became.

Never thought of fairytales and
bridges
The queen of my heart that you
became.
Millions of people with millions
of heart
But a heart of mine that you
became.
You when I'm wide open and
when I close my eyes
The center of my world that you
became.
All and everything was going
well
Then the target of evil that me
and you became.

It's trying to perish and severe
the bond
A bond which when me and you
became.
The silent tremors my heart feels
now
The fragments of memories in me
that you became.
They reside in me now and
forever
For once it was beautiful when
the life of mine that you became.
You are my everything that I
dreamt of
My past, present and future that
you became.

Crescent of the Darkest Night

When the crescent appears in the
darkest night
When my soul dwells upon the
slightest twilight
The fragile fragments of dimmed
memories
Seemed too vivid to my
unconscious sensories
Though I shall seek the path
away from you

My soul trembles as it is forced
to restrain from you
I desire that my heart wasn't
aflame
It lured snakes and lizards to
blame
Although you accept fate as your
aid
Stays behind scars of memories
once made
Fumed are they trapped in
jealousy
Dismayed their intentions of
fallacy
But would you ever care to
ponder

Of the act they display somber

Hence lies fears under my weary

eyes

Beneath those darkest of the

nights

A Few Questions

A few questions, about us, and you,

Do you still recall those times, or lie about them too?

Promises till the moon, now feel like a distant tune,

What was your takeaway? What did you leave?

Some questions to dismay, a hundred griefs to grieve,

*What would I validate? A million
lies you believed,
Sacrifices, trials, pain, and more,
Abundance of lies you believed,
in vain, I adore.*

*You were my light once, now my
darkness is you,
My days bright once, my dreams
are now you,
Until when will I suffer? Until
when will I mourn?
Reminisce of yours, still flutter, a
bittersweet pain that remains.*

The Lord blessed me again, with peace of sanity,
Awaiting your presence no more, yours beloved, and my immaturity,
A struggle for negligence, a few questions, yet to be answered,
Fragments of what we had, now scattered, guilt, loss, and thoughts silenced.

Endearment of mine still remains, a lingering pain,
A reminder of what we were, a memory that refuses to wane.

Love, A Mere Deceit

She said love's a lie, a mere
deceit,
I prayed you'd know love's sweet
heat.

May someone tear you two apart,
Then you'll roam from street to
street,
You'll chant their name, repeat
and repeat,
Then you'll say, "Love's true, it's

sweet."

A single drop of love, so deep,
Can drown the world, so soundly
sleep.
I've thirsted long, now I'm
submerged,
In love's vast ocean, I'm
deranged.

I long to steal you, make you
mine,
But stealing, love, you've never
taught me, fine.
Without your thought, my eyes

can't blink,
A storm within my heart does
think.

Why are we bound by these
chains so tight?
Entangled in this love's endless
night?
Your thought is sweet, I must
confess,
But love has taught me how to
bless.

Togetherness longed, a hope he
held,

But estrangement was what he felt.

What if.....

What if

You somehow reminisce about
me
The passionate pain to long for
me
You then ask pathways to fireflies

Then talk to clouds far in the
skies
The sweet breeze which will
guide you
The pinnacle of time will abide

you

What if
Melancholy to my absence,
adoring me
Rustling of silenced memories,
captivates you
I wish you knew of the verity
surrounding me
Would you endure the torment,
instills you
I wish you knew of the falsity
surrounding me
Venomous yet honeyed, words
that sew

What if

*I ponder often what would you
do
Believe me a liar, i accept
unexecuted crime
perhaps my love isnt ample
I wonder often that would you
knew
Trust my desire, words hardly
rhyme
Lonely i dwell as an apostle
Awaiting for your appearance, i
pray
Reminiscing about you, i pray*

I LOVED YOU

I loved you
From the time I saw you
Till the time you left me
I loved you
Used to gaze at you
From the corner of my eyes
I loved you
From the bottom of my heart
To the soul of you
I loved you
Adored every movement of yours
Quickness, grace and swiftness

I loved you
The tone of your voice
Melody flowing through the air
I loved you
Blinking and careful stare
Your eyes seeing me with care
I loved you
Beautiful calm breathes rhythmic
Followed by a hug and a mimic
I loved you
Your hand in mine clasped
Together when we walked
I loved you
Not for what you say now
But for what you said then
I loved you

Promises and trust are fake?

Dreams and reality fake?

I loved you

A bond broken up

A relation shattered

I loved you

Give me answers to my questions

Why is your name the only thing

my heart mentions?

I loved you

Something to nothing

Even after everything?

I loved you

No words left to stitch

Across a poem of low pitch

I loved you

My heart burns like husk
From the dawn till dusk
I loved you
Maybe or maybe not
Single soul or two can't sought
I loved you
Terrible my words somehow
Writes a poem anyhow
I loved you
Just like a moon to its earth
And the icy flames in its hearth

Subtle life of a clover

At times i used to wonder

Don't you ever ponder?

The very thought of loving you

always made me bloom

Don't you ever ponder?

At times i used to look up to the

sky

after the harsh sun

I always waited for my moon to

gloom

Don't you ever ponder?

Remnants of your voice would
always linger
around my mind unconsciously
Don't you ever ponder?
Those passionate eyes of yours
would steal my vision
and would replace with yours
Those eyes that haven't seen you
for a while especially
Don't you ever ponder?
I dream of us with the
philosophy
of a day where there would be no
boundaries
Don't you ever ponder?
Hearts that are always connected

Every time when they beat
would find peace
Don't you ever ponder?
A friendship, A bond, The Love,
The Lover
Eons of happiness and that subtle
life of a clover

You and Me

You look at me smiling
I look back to you smiling
The way we exchange our gaze
With you my heart stays
Could it be a dream that I dream
about
Maybe my dream is you and all
about
I say why do I charm you
Unfortunately, I don't have any
answer too
Maybe it's just the way you are

In a galaxy of emptiness my
lovely star
I sometimes think you act
I don't know for the fact
But then you prove me wrong
Every time you grow so strong
What if there is someone who
constantly thinks
Solely about you of all the things
Never leave this void heart
It will crumble away apart

IF I WAS AN ARTIST

I admire at your presence
Only if was an artist
I would have stroke you with the
softest brush
Only if I was an artist
I want to behold your very
existence
Only if I was an artist
I would sketch you with the
smoothest pencil
Only if I was an artist

I want to keep you at my nerve
distance
Only if I was an artist
I would shade you with the
coolest color
Only if I was an artist
I want to melt in your hands
Only if I was an artist
I would draw you with the same
passionate heart
Only if I was an artist
You made me lose myself only to
be found as a better version of
myself
I would care you with the
proudest soul

Only if I was an artist
And gaze you often till my eyes
lose sight

IT'S BEEN A LONG TIME

It's been a long time
Tell me, have you waited?
We had some beautiful memories
Tell me, have you been
fascinated?
Those dreams that we sewed
together
The feeling of compassion
towards each other
Tell me, do you still feel
passionate?
Remember the day I saw you?

Amidst the crowd, the only
immaculate

It's been a long time
Tell me, do you still feel
infatuated?
Over the things which we never
told
And over those which we told
Are there things yet to be
accepted?

It's been a long time
Oh, how wonderful your voice
soothes my soul

And your gaze hugs me and
speaks oh my soul
It's been a long time

OH MY SOUL

I want to tell you, oh my soul

It is you who completes me all

I want to feel you, oh my soul

It is your presence that makes me

whole

I want to show you, oh my soul

It is your light which covers my

dark hole

I want to hear you, oh my soul

Your songs, your voice, your call

I want to see you, oh my soul

Your form, your rise, your fall

I want to touch you, oh my soul
Your existence, your aura, your
sole
I wonder how you exist in me, oh
my soul

Amidst the chaos

Amidst the chaos I stood still
I could hear those silent screams
Those sharp edged thoughts that
could kill
Seeing them shatter my dreams
Amidst the chaos I looked still
Eyes brimmed with paradoxical
memories
Contradicting although verity
still
As I ride along a soft breeze
One of my only companions

Amidst the chaos I stayed still
As I envision running animals
Yet everything seemed to never
fulfill
Guillotined emotions, were once
for you
Amidst the chaos now play still
Keeps me wake, and never sleeps
too

www.ingramcontent.com/pod-product-compliance
Lightning Source LLC
LaVergne TN
LVHW011055200726
843509LV00011B/1413